New Weight Watchers Freestyle Cookbook 2022

Jennifer Tucson

CONTENTS

Chapter 1: Breakfast

Majestic Green Hearty Smoothie

Prep Time: 10 minutes

Cooking Time: Nil

Number of Servings: 2

Smart Points: 1

Ingredients:

- 1 medium banana, ripe and sliced

- 2 tablespoons water

- 2 tablespoons fresh orange juice

- ½ cup baby spinach leaves

- 1 cup of frozen berries

Method:

1. Add all of the listed ingredients to your blender/food processor.

2. Blend the entire mixture until it resembles a smoothie texture.

3. Allow it to cool in the refrigerator.

4. Serve and have fun!

Nutritional Values (Per Serving)

- Calories: 321

- Fat: 11 g

- Saturated Fat: 2 g

- Carbohydrates: 55 g

- Fiber: 6 g

- Sodium: 64 mg

- Protein: 5 g

Tasty Avocado And Egg Toast

Prep Time: 10 minutes

Cooking Time: 5 minutes

Number of Servings: 4

Smart Points: 6

Ingredients:

- 2 large whole eggs
- 3 tablespoons avocado flesh, mashed
- Salt as needed
- Hot sauce as needed
- Fresh ground pepper to taste
- 2 and ½ slices of whole wheat bread
- Olive oil as needed

Method:

1. Take your bread slices and make a hole in the middle using a cookie cutter
2. Season avocado mash with salt and pepper
3. Take a skillet and place it over medium-low heat, grease with cooking spray
4. Place bread slices and a cut portion in the skillet
5. Break the egg into the hole of the bread, cook until the egg properly settles down, season with more salt and pepper

6. Flip and cook the other side

7. Once done, transfer to a plate

8. Top the egg with avocado mash, hot sauce, and crumble bread (made from the cut piece)

9. Enjoy

<u>**Nutritional Values (Per Serving)**</u>

- Calories: 229

- Fat: 23g

- Carbohydrates: 10g

- Protein: 12g

- Saturated Fat: 4g

- Sodium: 801mg

- Fiber: 2g

Oats And Apple Breakfast Meal

Prep Time: 10 minutes

Cooking Time: 20-30 minutes

Number of Servings: 3

Smart Points: 4

Ingredients:

- 2 cups oats

- 4 cups flour, whole wheat

- 1 cup raw honey

- Salt as needed

- 4 cups apples, diced

- ½ cup apple sauce

- ½ cup almond milk

- ½ tablespoon vanilla extract

- Pinch of baking soda

- ¾ tablespoon cinnamon

Method:

1. Combine all of the ingredients in a heat-resistant mixing bowl.

2. Open the top lid of an Instant Pot.

3. Pour 1 cup of water into the cooking pot and place the steamer basket/trivet inside.

4. Place the bowl on top of the basket/trivet.

5. Close the top lid and double-check that the valve is closed.

6. "MANUAL" should be selected "function of cooking Cooking time should be reduced to 20-25 minutes.

7. Allow the pressure to build up before cooking the ingredients for the specified amount of time.

8. Press •CANCEL when the cooking timer runs out, "then press the "NPP" button. For the next 8-10 minutes, the Instant Pot will slowly and naturally release the pressure.

9. Remove the top lid and open it. Serve the cooked mixture on plates.

10. Warm the dish before serving.

Nutritional Values (Per Serving)

- Calories:164
- Fat:45g
- Carbohydrates: 32g
- Fiber:4g
- Sodium :104mg
- Protein:3g

Mediterranean Egg Sandwich

Prep Time: 10 minutes

Cooking Time: 25 minutes

Number of Servings: 3

Smart Points: 20

Ingredients:

- ¼ cup egg whites

- Salt and pepper as needed

- 1 teaspoon butter

- 1 whole-grain seeded ciabatta roll

- 1 teaspoon of fresh herbs such as parsley, oregano, etc.

- ½ cup roasted tomatoes

- 1-2 slices cheese

- 1 tablespoon pesto

Roasted Tomatoes

- 10 ounces grape tomatoes

- 1 tablespoon extra virgin olive oil

- Salt and pepper to taste

Method:

1. Melt the butter until completely melted in a small nonstick skillet over medium heat. Season with salt and pepper to taste after adding the egg whites. Add a handful of fresh herbs on top. Cook, turning halfway through, for 3-4 minutes, or until the egg is done.

2. In the meantime, toast the Ciabatta bread in the toaster. Read it on both halves of the table after you're done. Place the egg on the bottom half of the sandwich roll, folding it in half if necessary, and top with the cheese. Close the roll by placing the roasted tomatoes on the top half. The aandwich aandwich aandwich aandwich aandwich

3. To make the roasted tomatoes, do the following: Preheat the oven to 400 degrees Fahrenheit (200 degrees Celsius). To prepare the tomatoes, split them in half lengthwise. Drizzle the olive oil over the mixture and place it on a baking sheet. It's time to put on your coat. Season well with salt and pepper and roast for about 20 minutes in the oven. The skin will appear wrinkled after the procedure is completed.

Nutritional Values (Per Serving)

- Calories: 458
- Fat: 24 g
- Saturated Fat: 8 g
- Carbohydrates: 10 g
- Fiber: 3 g
- Sodium: 251 mg
- Protein: 21 g

Greek Yogurt Pancakes

Prep Time: 15 minutes

Cooking Time: 15 minutes

Number of Servings: 6

Smart Points: 10

Ingredients:

- 1 and ½ cups Greek Yogurt, plain- Non Fat
- ½ cup milk
- ½ cup blueberries
- 1 tablespoons butter, unsalted, melted
- 2 whole eggs
- 1 teaspoon baking soda
- ¼ cup sugar
- ¼ cup all-purpose flour
- ¼ teaspoon salt
- 1 teaspoon baking powder

Method:

1. Combine the flour, salt, baking powder, and baking soda in a large mixing bowl.
2. Whisk together the sugar and butter and the eggs, Greek yogurt, and milk in a separate dish until smooth.

3. In a separate bowl, combine the Greek yogurt and flour mixture from Step 1. I like to let the batter rest for 20 minutes to ensure completely smooth and textured. Combine the blueberries and half of the cake batter in a separate bowl. (Alternatively, half of the cake batter and the blueberries could be folded in.)

4. Before cooking, spray or brush a pancake griddle with nonstick butter spray or real butter. A quarter of a cup of batter Cook until the bubbles on the surface burst and small holes appear. Lift the edges of each pancake to ensure that golden berries cover the bottom. Flip the cake with a wide spatula and cook the other side until lightly browned. Allow the pancakes to cool on a baking sheet until ready to serve.

5. Fill each half of the pancake with Greek yogurt and mixed fruit for a delicious way to end the meal (blueberries, raspberries, and blackberries).

Nutritional Values (Per Serving)

- Calories: 258
- Fat: 8 g
- Saturated Fat: 2 g
- Carbohydrates: 7 g
- Fiber: 1 g
- Sodium: 124 mg
- Protein: 12 g

Greek Omelet Casserole

Prep Time: 15 minutes

Cooking Time: 35 minutes

Number of Servings: 6

Smart Points: 6

Ingredients:

- 8 ounces fresh spinach

- 2 cups whole milk

- 12 whole large eggs

- 12 ounces artichoke salad

- 2 garlic cloves, minced

- 1 teaspoon dried oregano

- 1 tablespoon fresh chopped dill

- 5 ounces sun-dried tomato feta cheese, crumbled

- 4 teaspoons olive oil

- 1 teaspoon salt

- 1 teaspoon lemon pepper

Method:

1. Preheat oven to 375°F (190°C). Chopped finely, prepare the fresh herbs and artichoke salad.

2. 2.1 tablespoon of olive oil, to taste, in a skillet over medium heat. Saute the spinach and garlic for approximately 3 minutes, or until the spinach has wilted.

3. Coat a 9x13-inch baking dish and evenly arrange the spinach and artichoke salad using cooking spray.

4. Whirl together the eggs, milk, herbs, salt, and lemon pepper in a medium mixing bowl.

5. Pour the egg mixture over the veggies and, if preferred, sprinkle with feta cheese. Preheat the oven to 350°F and bake the cake for 35-40 minutes, or firm in the middle.

Nutritional Values (Per Serving)

- Calories: 186
- Fat: 13 g
- Saturated Fat: 2 g
- Carbohydrates: 13 g
- Fiber: 2 g
- Sodium: 245 mg
- Protein: 10 g

Crunchy Oat Bars

Prep Time: 10 minutes

Cooking Time: 30 minutes

Number of Servings: 6

Ingredients:

- 2 cups oats
- Non-stick spray
- 1 cup unsweetened coconut, shredded
- ½ teaspoon salt
- ¼ cup raw turbinado sugar
- ¼ cup flaxseed
- ¼ cup toasted sesame seeds
- 2 tablespoons psyllium powder
- ¾ cup butter
- ¼ cup honey

Method:

1. Preheat your oven to 350 degrees F

2. Take an 11x7 cake pan and grease well

3. Take a large-sized bowl and add oats, coconut, salt, sugar, flaxseed, psyllium, and sesame

4. Take a small pan and place it over low heat

5. Add butter and honey, let it melt

6. Add the honey mix to the bowl with dry ingredients

7. Mix well

8. Transfer to prepared baking pan and press them firmly into a fine layer

9. Bake for 25 minutes, remove and cut into 9 bars

10. Serve and enjoy!

Nutritional Values (Per Serving)

- Calories: 365

- Fat: 14 g

- Saturated Fat: 3 g

- Carbohydrates: 55 g

- Fiber: 5 g

- Sodium: 79 mg

- Protein: 9 g

Exotic Almond Pancake

Number of Servings: 6

Prep Time: 10 minutes

Cooking Time: 10 minutes

SmartPoints: 3

Ingredients:

- 6 whole eggs
- ¼ cup almonds, toasted
- 2 ounces cocoa chocolate
- 1/3 cup coconut, shredded
- 1 teaspoon almond extract
- ½ teaspoon baking powder
- ¼ cup of coconut oil
- ¼ cup stevia
- 1 cup almond milk
- Cooking spray as needed
- Pinch of salt

Method:

1. Take a bowl and add coconut flour, stevia, salt, baking powder, coconut, and gently stir

2. Add coconut oil, eggs, almond milk, almond extract and stir well

3. Add chocolate, almond and whisk well

4. Take a pan and place it over medium heat, add 2 tablespoons batter, spread into a circle

5. Cook until golden and flip, transfer to pan

6. Repeat with remaining batter

7. Serve and enjoy!

Nutritional Values (Per Serving)

- Calories: 266

- Fat: 13g

- Carbohydrates: 10g

- Protein: 11g

- Saturated Fat: 2g

- Sodium: 242mg

- Fiber: 1g

Homemade Strawberry Bruschetta Meal

Number of Servings: 6

Prep Time: 10 minutes

Cooking Time: 10 minutes

SmartPoints: 5

Ingredients:

- 4 tablespoons reduced-fat cream cheese

- 5 tablespoons light brown sugar

- 2 teaspoons lemon juice

- 3 cups fresh strawberries, diced

- 4 thick slices of whole wheat bread

Method:

1. In a toaster, toast the bread.

2. Meanwhile, in a large skillet, heat the oil over high heat. Cook, stirring constantly, until the sugar melts and the mixture begins to bubble, about 30 seconds to 1 minute.

3. Stir in the strawberries for another 30 seconds to 1 minute, or until the juices have released and the berries are thoroughly heated.

4. On each piece of toast, spread 1 tbsp light cream cheese. Add the warm berries on top.

Nutritional Values (Per Serving)

- Calories: 166

- Fat: 38g

- Carbohydrates: 5g

- Protein: 4g

- Saturated Fat: 2g

- Sodium: 214mg

- Fiber: 0.8g

Blueberry And Ricotta Buttermilk Pancake

Number of Servings: 6

Prep Time: 10 minutes

Cooking Time: 10 minutes

SmartPoints: 5=4

Ingredients:

- 1 teaspoon vanilla extract

- 1 teaspoon lemon juice

- 1 teaspoon fresh lemon zest, grated

- ½ cup part-skim ricotta cheese

- ½ cup liquid egg substitute

- ½ teaspoon fresh nutmeg, grated

- ½ cup fresh blueberries

- 1/3 cup water

- 1 cup whole wheat buttermilk pancake mix

Method:

1. In a small bowl, combine whole-wheat flour and nutmeg.

2. In a large mixing bowl, whisk the ricotta, egg substitute, vanilla extract, lemon zest, and juice until smooth. Combine the dry and wet ingredients and stir until

just combined. If the batter is too thick, add a teaspoon of water at a time until the desired consistency is achieved.

3. Place a large nonstick skillet over medium heat and spray with nonfat, butter-flavored cooking spray.

4. Pour the batter into the pan for two 4-inch pancakes, top with blueberries, and cook until the edges are dry and bubbles form about 2 minutes. Cook for another 2 minutes on the other side, or until golden brown.

5. Using the remaining batter and berries, repeat the process, adjusting the heat as needed to avoid burning.

Nutritional Values (Per Serving)

- Calories: 163
- Fat: 26g
- Carbohydrates: 11g
- Protein: 4g
- Saturated Fat: 5g
- Sodium: 251mg
- Fiber: 1g

The Copycat Spicy Sandwich

Number of Servings: 4

Prep Time: 10 minutes + 60 minutes marinate

Cooking Time: 10 minutes

SmartPoints: 4

Ingredients:

- 1 tomato, sliced
- 1 head romaine lettuce
- 4 lite hamburger buns
- ¼ cup 1% milk
- 2 whole eggs
- ¼ teaspoon cayenne pepper
- 1 teaspoon paprika
- 1 teaspoon garlic powder
- 1 teaspoon garlic powder
- ½ cup flour
- ¼ cup pickle juice
- 2 chicken breasts, split in half, lengthwise

Method:

1. Using a sharp knife, cut your chicken breasts in half lengthwise. Place them in a zip lock bag with the pickle juice. Allow 1 hour in the fridge to marinate.

2. Combine the flour and spices in a shallow dish. In a different shallow dish, whisk together the eggs and milk.

3. With a tong, remove the chicken breasts from the bag and dip them first in the eggs and milk, then in the flour mixture.

4. Spray the top side of the chicken breast with cooking spray before placing it in the air fryer basket. Preheat the air fryer to 400 degrees Fahrenheit. Preheat the oven to 350°F and set the timer for 7 minutes.

5. When the 7 minutes are up, remove the chicken from the air fryer and flip it. Close the basket and re-spray. Set the timer for 4 minutes more. Serve the chicken with lettuce and tomatoes on a bun.

Nutritional Values (Per Serving)

- Calories: 222
- Fat: 31g
- Carbohydrates: 21g
- Protein: 5g
- Saturated Fat: 2g
- Sodium: 344mg
- Fiber: 2g

Chapter 2: Chicken And Poultry

Supreme Balsamic Chicken

Prep Time: 10 minutes

Cooking Time: 20 minutes

Number of Servings: 3

SmartPoints: 3

Ingredients:

- 3 chicken breast, boneless and skinless
- Salt and pepper to taste
- ¼ cup all-purpose flour
- 2/3 cup low-fat chicken broth
- 1 and ½ teaspoon of corn starch
- ½ cup low sugar raspberry preserve
- 1 and ½ tablespoons balsamic vinegar

Method:

1. Cut the chicken into bite-sized portions and season with salt and pepper

2. Dredge the meat into flour and shake off excess

3. Take a non-stick skillet and place it over medium heat

4. Add chicken and cook for 15 minutes, turning once halfway through

5. Remove cooked chicken and transfer to a plate

6. Add cornstarch, chicken broth, raspberry preserve into the skillet and stir in balsamic vinegar (keep the heat on medium)

7. Transfer the cooked chicken to the skillet

8. Cook for 15 minutes more, making sure to turn once

9. Serve and enjoy!

Nutritional Values (Per Serving)

- Calories: 546
- Fat: 35 g
- Saturated Fat: 7 g
- Carbohydrates: 11 g
- Fiber: 3 g
- Sodium: 930 mg
- Protein: 44 g

Juicy Lemon And Pepper Chicken

Prep Time: 10 minutes

Cooking Time: 15 minutes

Number of Servings: 4

SmartPoints: 3

Ingredients:

- 1 tablespoon olive oil

- 4 cups skinless chicken cutlets

- 2 whole eggs

- ½ cup panko

- 1 tablespoon lemon pepper

- Salt and pepper to taste

- 5 cups green beans

- 4 tablespoons parmesan cheese

- 1 teaspoon garlic powder

Method:

1. Preheat your oven to 360 Degrees F

2. Take a bowl and stir in seasoning, parmesan. lemon pepper, garlic powder, panko

3. Whisk eggs in another bowl

4. Coat cutlets in eggs and press into panko mix

5. Transfer coated chicken to a parchment-lined a baking sheet

6. Toss the beans in oil. pepper, and salt, lay them on the side of the baking sheet

7. Bake for 15 minutes

8. Enjoy!

Nutritional Values (Per Serving)

- Calories: 300

- Fat:10g

- Carbohydrates: 10g

- Protein: 43g

- Saturated Fat: 3g

- Sodium: 945mg

- Fiber: 2g

Chicken And Asparagus Platter

Number of Servings: 3

Prep Time: 10 minutes

Cooking Time: 25-30 minutes

SmartPoints: 3

Ingredients:

- ½ pounds asparagus, trimmed
- 2 pounds chicken breasts, cut in half to make 4 thin pieces
- 4 sundried tomatoes, cut into strips
- 8 provolone cheese slices
- Salt and pepper to taste

Method:

1. Preheat the oven to 400 degrees F and grease a large baking sheet well.
2. Arrange chicken breasts and asparagus on a sheet pan, then top with sundried tomatoes.
3. Season to taste with salt and pepper, then place in the oven.
4. Remove from oven after 25 minutes of baking.
5. Bake for 3 minutes with provolone cheese slices on top.
6. Dish up, serve, and have fun!

Nutritional Values (Per Serving)

- Calories: 322

- Fat: 15g

- Carbohydrates: 3g

- Protein: 40g

- Saturated Fat: 3g

- Sodium: 399mg

- Fiber: 1g

Sheet Pan Ala Brussels And Chicken

Prep Time: 10 minutes

Cooking Time: 30-35 minutes

Number of Servings: 4

SmartPoints: 1

Ingredients:

- 1 pound sweet potatoes, cut into ½ inch wedges

- 2 tablespoons extra-virgin olive oil

- /34 teaspoon salt

- ¾ teaspoon ground pepper

- 4 cups Brussels sprouts, quartered

- 1 and ¼ pounds boneless, skinless chicken thighs, trimmed

- ½ teaspoon ground cumin

- ½ teaspoon dried thyme

- 3 tablespoons sherry vinegar

Method:

1. Preheat your oven to 425 degrees F

2. Take a large-sized bowl and add potatoes, a quarter teaspoon of salt, pepper, and 1 tablespoon of oil

3. Spread the mix over a rimmed baking sheet

4. Transfer to oven and roast for 15 minutes

5. Take a bowl and add Brussels, a quarter teaspoon of salt, pepper, and remaining oil

6. Pour the mix over potatoes (on the baking sheet)

7. Sprinkle the remaining teaspoon of salt and pepper, thyme, cumin over chicken

8. Put on top of veggies

9. Roast for 10-15 minutes until the veggies are tender and chicken is cooked well

10. Transfer chicken to serving platter and serve with veggies

11. Enjoy!

Nutritional Values (Per Serving)

- Calories: 351

- Fat: 15 g

- Saturated Fat: 3 g

- Carbohydrates: 25 g

- Fiber: 1 g

- Sodium: 607 mg

- Protein: 29 g

The Mushroom And Pear Chicken Extravaganza

Prep Time: 10 minutes

Cooking Time: 15 minutes

Number of Servings: 1

SmartPoints: 2

Ingredients:

- 2 pounds chicken breast, boneless
- 1 cup mushroom, sliced
- 15 ounces canned pears, sliced
- ½ tablespoon brown sugar
- ½ teaspoon black pepper
- 1 teaspoon salt
- 2 tablespoons balsamic vinegar

Method:

1. Add listed ingredients to Instant Pot

2. Mix well

3. Lock lid and cook on HIGH pressure for 15 minutes

4. Release pressure over 10 minutes

5. Open the lid and serve

6. Enjoy!

Nutritional Values (Per Serving)

- Calories: 503

- Fat: 17 g

- Saturated Fat: 5 g

- Carbohydrates: 18 g

- Fiber: 2 g

- Sodium: 267 mg

- Protein: 25 g

Meaty Chicken Parm Cutlet

Prep Time: 10 minutes

Cooking Time: 15 minutes

Number of Servings: 1

SmartPoints: 3

Ingredients:

- 4 boneless chicken breast
- ¼ teaspoon pepper
- ¼ teaspoon ground black pepper
- ½ teaspoon garlic powder
- 1 teaspoon dried parsley
- 1/8 teaspoon paprika
- 2 tablespoons seasonal Italian crumbs
- ¼ cup parmesan cheese, grated

Method:

1. Preheat the oven to 400 degrees Fahrenheit (200 degrees Celsius).
2. Combine cheese, seasoning, and crumbs in a resealable plastic bag.
3. Everything should be well shaken.
4. Transfer the mixture to a bowl and dip your chicken breasts into it, making sure to coat both sides thoroughly.

5. Place the seasoned breasts on top of a non-stick baking sheet.

6. Bake the chicken for about 25 minutes, or until thoroughly cooked.

7. Serve immediately!

Nutritional Values (Per Serving)

- Calories: 669

- Fat: 43g

- Carbohydrates: 3 6g

- Protein: 34g

- Saturated fat: 10 g

- Fiber: 2 g

- Sodium: 258 mg

Slow Cooked Teriyaki Chicken And Pineapple

Prep Time: 10 minutes

Cooking Time: 6 hours 10 minutes

Number of Servings: 4

SmartPoints: 4

Ingredients:

- 2 and ½ pounds boneless chicken thighs

- 1 can pineapple chunks, drained

- ¾ cup teriyaki sauce

- ¼ cup green onion, chopped

- 2 tablespoons tapioca

Method:

1. Ideal Slow Cooker Size: 4-Quart.

2. Coat the slow cooker with nonstick cooking spray.

3. Place the chicken thighs in the slow cooker.

4. Stir together the pineapple, teriyaki sauce, green onion, and tapioca in a bowl. Pour the mixture over the chicken.

5. Cover and cook on LOW for 6 to 8 hours or on HIGH for 3 to 4 hours, or until the chicken is fork-tender.

<u>Nutritional Values (Per Serving)</u>

- Calories: 240

- Fat: 51g

- Carbohydrates: 16g

- Protein: 20g

- Saturated fat: 5 g

- Fiber: 2 g

- Sodium: 351 mg

Lovely Chicken Alfredo Pizza

Prep Time: 10 minutes

Cooking Time: 5-10 minutes

Number of Servings: 4

SmartPoints: 3

Ingredients:

- ¾ cup part-skim mozzarella cheese

- 1 cup leftover chicken

- ½ cup light alfredo sauce

- 1 cup self-rising flour

- 1 cup non-fat Greek yogurt

Method:

1. To make the crust, whisk together the flour and Greek yogurt in a medium mixing bowl until a dough forms. You can shape it with your hands or with a scraper.

2. Preheat the oven to 400 degrees Fahrenheit.

3. On a flat surface, sift the flour. Over a lightly floured surface, roll out pizza dough into a 12-inch round, leaving a larger rim around the edge of the dough for the crust.

4. Spread 1/2 cup alfredo sauce on the pizza dough, leaving room for the crust. Then add chicken and cheese to the rest of the pizza.

5. Preheat oven to 400°F and bake for 14 minutes.

6. Finish with a sprig of parsley.

<u>Nutritional Values (Per Serving)</u>

- Calories: 142

- Fat: 10g

- Carbohydrates: 15g

- Protein: 14g

- Saturated fat: 2 g

- Fiber: 2 g

- Sodium: 377 mg

Blackened Chicken Alfredo Meal

Prep Time: 10 minutes

Cooking Time: 20-30 minutes

Number of Servings: 4

SmartPoints: 10

Ingredients:

- 2 small chicken breasts

- 2 teaspoons Daks original red

- 8 ounces spaghetti noodles

- 2 tablespoons light butter

- 2 teaspoons garlic cloves, chopped

- 1 cup fat-free half and half

- ½ cup parmesan cheese

Method:

1. Two chicken breasts should be cut in half lengthwise. Original red seasoning or Cajun seasoning can be used to season chicken breasts. In a nonstick skillet, brown the chicken breasts. Cook the chicken for a few minutes on one side before flipping it. Time: 3–4 minutes Cook until the chicken is cooked through. Take the chicken out of the pan.

2. Drain the noodles after cooking them according to the package directions.

3. In a medium nonstick saucepan, melt two tablespoons of butter and add the garlic. Add the half-and-half and the parmesan cheese. Allow to simmer until the sauce has thickened, whisking constantly. Add the drained noodles and mix well.

4. This recipe serves four people. 1 1/2 cup serving size

Nutritional Values (Per Serving)

- Calories: 493

- Fat: 12g

- Carbohydrates: 46g

- Protein: 45g

- Saturated fat: 26g

- Fiber: 1 g

- Sodium: 420 mg

Exotic Chicken Cordon Blue

Prep Time: 10 minutes

Cooking Time: 20-30 minutes

Number of Servings: 4

SmartPoints: 5

Ingredients:

- Salt and pepper to taste
- 2 whole eggs
- 1/3 cup parmesan cheese
- 1/3 cup bread crumbs
- 4 slices ham
- 4 slices Swiss Cheese
- 4 skinless, boneless chicken breast

Method:

1. Chicken breasts should be pounded until they are very thin. This step can be done with a rolling pin or a meat mallet. Using salt and pepper, season the chicken. On top of the chicken, place one slice of ham and one slice of Swiss cheese and roll it up into a small bundle.

2. If necessary, secure the chicken breasts with toothpicks.

3. The chicken should be dipped in the egg, then in the bread crumbs and parmesan cheese. Rep with the rest of the chicken breasts. Place each chicken in the air fryer basket and cook for 8 to 10 minutes at 350 degrees.

4. When the chicken is no longer pink in the middle of the temperature reaches 165 degrees, it is done.

5. Serve with mashed potatoes or a salad on the side.

Nutritional Values (Per Serving)

- Calories: 319
- Fat: 12g
- Carbohydrates: 10g
- Protein: 34g
- Saturated fat: 2g
- Fiber: 2 g
- Sodium: 245 mg

Chapter 3: Snacks And Appetizers

Fancy Pineapple Salsa

Prep Time: 10 minutes

Cooking Time: Nil

Number of Servings: 4

SmartPoints: 0

Ingredients:

- ½ pineapple, diced
- 2 teaspoons fire jalapeno, chopped
- 2 green onion, sliced
- 1 teaspoon ground cumin
- 2 tablespoons lime juice, fresh
- Salt and pepper to taste

Method:

1. Cut the outer skin of your pineapple by cutting off the ends

2. Stand it on one side and cut the sides flat

3. Slice the pineapple into ¼ inch planks down the side

4. Cut the planks into dices and add them to a bowl

5. Chop the jalapeno and cut off the stem

6. Slice them lengthwise and take them out of the membrane and deseed them

7. Add them to the bowl with pineapple

8. Slice the green onion into thin layers and add them to the bowl

9. Add cumin, lime juice, cilantro, pepper, and salt and toss well

10. Serve and enjoy!

Nutritional Values (Per Serving)

- Calories: 380

- Fat: 18 g

- Saturated Fat: 4 g

- Carbohydrates: 47 g

- Fiber: 2 g

- Sodium: 205 mg

- Protein: 10 g

Divine Greek Salad Sushi Delight

Prep Time: 10 minutes

Cooking Time: Nil

Number of Servings: 10 rolls

SmartPoints: 2

Ingredients:

- ½ cup Plain Greek Yogurt

- 1 cucumber

- 1 garlic clove, minced

- 2 teaspoons lemon juice

- ½ bell pepper, diced

- 1 teaspoon fresh dill, chopped

- Salt and pepper to taste

- ¼ cup crumbled feta cheese

- ¼ cup red onion, diced

Method:

1. Using a mandolin or a vegetable peeler, slice off the ends of the cucumber and peel thin slices down the length of the cucumber. Lay the slices out on several layers of paper towels, then top with a few more. Allow the tzatziki sauce to dry and chill while you're working on it.

2. Tzatziki: To make tzatziki, whisk together the yogurt, lemon juice, garlic, dill, salt, and pepper in a mixing bowl.

3. Spread tztziki on a cucumber slice and roll it up. Finish with flour, feta, pepper, and onion sprinkling. Make a cylinder out of the dough and secure it with a toothpick. Continue to cook until you've used up all of your ingredients.

Nutritional Values (Per Serving)

- Calories: 255
- Fat: 20 g
- Saturated Fat: 5 g
- Carbohydrates: 25 g
- Fiber: 2 g
- Sodium: 251 mg
- Protein: 9 g

Herbed Up Lovely Lemon Orzo Salad

Prep Time: 10 minutes

Cooking Time: 15 minutes

Number of Servings: 4

SmartPoints: 2

Ingredients:

- 2 large handfuls of fresh baby spinach, chopped

- 1-2 lemons, zested and juiced

- 1 cup roughly chopped fresh mint leaves

- 1 cup fresh basil leaves, roughly chopped

- ½ a small red onion, diced

- Salt and pepper as needed

- ½ cup crumbled goat cheese

- ¼ cup olive oil

- 15 ounces chickpeas, rinsed and drained

- 1 English cucumber, diced

- 12 ounces uncooked orzo

Method:

1. Cook the pasta according to package instructions in a large stockpot of salted water until al dente. 2. Drain the pasta and rinse it well with cold water in a colander until it cools. Fill a large mixing bowl halfway with the paste.

2. Combine the remaining ingredients in a mixing basin (along with the cheese, if you like). Toss until all of the ingredients are spread evenly. Before serving, taste and season with a few liberal pinches of salt and pepper to taste. (For each batch, I used around 1 teaspoon of salt and pepper.)

3. Add additional lemon juice to taste if you want a more lemony salad. (This is one of my favorites.) As quickly as feasible, serve. Cover and store it in the refrigerator for up to 3 days.

Nutritional Values (Per Serving)

- Calories: 338
- Fat: 25 g
- Saturated Fat: 10 g
- Carbohydrates: 10 g
- Fiber: 2 g
- Sodium: 351 mg
- Protein: 2 g

Thoughtful Bistro Lunchbox

Prep Time: 10 minutes

Cooking Time: 5 minutes

Number of Servings: 1

SmartPoints: 2

Ingredients:

- ½ cup grapes

- 1 pound Red, Seedless Grapes

- 2 large radishes, halved

- 4 slices English cucumber

- 1 slice prosciutto

- 1 mozzarella stick, halved

- 2 breadsticks, halved

- 2 dates

Method:

1. One Prosecco bottle is cut half lengthwise and wrapped around each cheese portion.

2. In a 4-cup split resealable container, combine the wrapped cheese, breadsticks, dates, grapes, and radish (or cucumber).

3. Refrigerate the dish until it's time to serve it.

4. Refrigerate for up to one day if made ahead of time.

Nutritional Values (Per Serving)

- Calories: 351

- Fat: 29 g

- Saturated Fat: 8 g

- Carbohydrates: 12 g

- Fiber: 3 g

- Sodium: 251 mg

- Protein: 7 g

Faithful Scrambled Eggs

Number of Servings: 2

Prep Time: 10 minutes

Cooking Time: 10 minutes

SmartPoints: 2

Ingredients:

- 1 teaspoon water

- 3 whole eggs

- Salt and pepper to taste

- ½ cup feta cheese, crumbled

- 1 tablespoon butter, melted

Method:

1. Place a skillet or a pan over medium heat.

2. Add the butter and allow it to melt.

3. Whisk together the water and eggs in a mixing bowl, then pour the mixture into the pan.

4. Stir in the feta cheese and stir gently until the eggs are scrambled.

5. Season to taste with salt and pepper.

6. Enjoy!

<u>Nutritional Values (Per Serving)</u>

- Calories: 183

- Fat: 15g

- Carbohydrates: 1g

- Protein: 10g

- Saturated Fat: 2g

- Sodium: 200mg

- Fiber: 1g

Simple And Easy Green Soup

Number of Servings: 3

Prep Time: 10 minutes

Cooking Time: 10-15 minutes

SmartPoints: 3

Ingredients:

- 1 cauliflower head, florets separated

- 1 white onion, chopped

- 1 bay leaf, crushed

- 5 ounces watercress

- 1-quart vegetable stock

- 1 cup of coconut milk

- 7 ounces of spinach leaves

- ¼ cup ghee

- Handful of parsley

- Salt and pepper to taste

Method:

1. Take a pot and place it over medium-high heat, add garlic, onion and stir cook for 4 minutes

2. Add cauliflower, bay leaf, and cook for 5 minutes

3. Add watercress, spinach and cook for 3 minutes

4. Add stock, salt, and pepper, bring to a boil

5. Add coconut milk, stir well and use a hand blender to blend well

6. Divide into bowls, serve and enjoy!

Nutritional Values (Per Serving)

- Calories: 230

- Fat: 34g

- Carbohydrates: 5g

- Protein: 7g

- Saturated Fat: 6g

- Sodium: 717mg

- Fiber: 3g

Walnut And Raisin Granola Bowl

Number of Servings: 3

Prep Time: 10 minutes

Cooking Time: 8 minutes

SmartPoints: 3

Ingredients:

- ¼ teaspoon salt

- Zest of 1 orange, grated

- 1 teaspoon cinnamon, grounded

- 1 tablespoon canola oil

- ¼ cup coconut, flaked and sweetened

- ¼ cup raw wheat germ

- 3 cups oats, old fashioned and rolled

- ½ cup raisins

- 1/3 cup raw pumpkin seeds

- 1/3 cup walnuts, chopped

1. Method:

2. Preheat the oven to 300 degrees Fahrenheit.

3. Using a nonstick spray, coat an a10.5xl5.5-inch jelly-roll pan.

4. In a large mixing bowl, combine all ingredients except the raisins.

5. Spread the mixture evenly in the prepared baking pan.

6. 25 minutes in the oven

7. Stir in the raisins and set the pan on a wire rack to cool completely.

8. Can be kept for up to a month in an airtight container.

9. Serve and have fun!

Nutritional Values (Per Serving)

- Calories: 178

- Fat: 8 g

- Carbohydrate: 22 g

- Protein: 5 g

- Saturated fat: 1 g

- Fiber: 3 g

- Sodium: 8 mg

The Perfect Weight Watchers Banana Pancake

Number of Servings: 3

Prep Time: 10 minutes

Cooking Time: 20-30 minutes

SmartPoints: 3

Ingredients:

- 1 cup oat flour
- ½ teaspoon baking powder
- 1 teaspoon vanilla extract
- 2 whole eggs
- 2 ripe bananas

Method:

1. Mash the ripe bananas in a bowl.

2. Oil a nonstick griddle or skillet and set to medium-high heat (about 350-375°F).

3. Use a 1 /8 cup for measuring batter on a griddle prepared with butter. Cook pancakes for 2-3 minutes or until bubbles start to form in the center and the edges are dry and golden on one side and flip - then cook for another 1-2 minutes.

4. Repeat until all the batter is used up. Add your toppings of choice and enjoy.

<u>Nutritional Values (Per Serving)</u>

- Calories: 160

- Fat: 3 g

- Carbohydrate: 27 g

- Protein: 3 g

- Saturated fat: 1 g

- Fiber: 1 g

- Sodium: 245 mg

The Zero Point Cheesecake

Number of Servings: 8

Prep Time: 10 minutes

Cooking Time: 30-40 minutes

SmartPoints: 0

Ingredients:

- 3 tablespoons sugar substitute

- 1 tablespoons vanilla extract

- 1 small box instant sugar Cheesecake pudding flavor

- 3 whole eggs

- 3 cups Fat-Free Greek Yogurt

Method:

1. In a mixing bowl, add eggs, sugar substitute, and vanilla extract and beat well.

2. Add yogurt and pudding and mix well.

3. Pour into a lightly greased pie dish.

4. Bake on 3 50 degrees for 3 0 min.

5. Chill for at least 2 hours or overnight before eating.

Nutritional Values (Per Serving)

- Calories: 162

- Fat: 7 g

- Carbohydrate: 17 g

- Protein: 9 g

- Saturated fat: 2 g

- Fiber: 1 g

- Sodium: 300 mg

Sheet Pan Chicken Fajitas

Number of Servings: 8

Prep Time: 10 minutes

Cooking Time: 30-40 minutes

SmartPoints: 1

Ingredients:

- 2 teaspoons fajita seasoning
- Cooking spray
- 1 onion, halved
- 1 red bell pepper, sliced
- 1 green pepper, sliced
- 2-3 small-medium chicken breasts, sliced

Method:

1. Preheat the oven to 400 degrees.
2. 2 teaspoons fajita seasoning, onion, peppers, and chicken in a small bowl. To combine, whisk everything together thoroughly.
3. On a large sheet pan, combine the chicken and vegetables. Cooking spray should be used.
4. Distribute evenly.

5. Bake for 25-30 minutes, or until the chicken is cooked and the vegetables are soft and crispy on the edges.

6. Serve the meal by dividing it into 6 portions.

7. Enjoy!

Nutritional Values (Per Serving)

- Calories: 200

- Fat: 4 g

- Carbohydrate: 2 g

- Protein: 6 g

- Saturated fat: 1 g

- Fiber: 1 g

- Sodium: 258 mg

Chapter 4: Meat Recipes

Divine Onion Pork Cutlets

Prep Time: 10 minutes

Cooking Time: 10 minutes

Number of Servings: 4

SmartPoints: 4

Ingredients:

- 1 tablespoon olive oil
- 2 pork cutlets
- 1 bell pepper, deveined and sliced
- 1 Spanish onion, chopped
- 2 garlic cloves, minced
- ½ teaspoon hot sauce
- ½ teaspoon mustard
- ½ teaspoon paprika
- Salt and pepper to taste

Method:

1. Take a large saucepan, add olive oil and place it over medium-high heat

2. Let it heat up, add pork cutlets and fry for 3-4 minutes until golden and crispy on both sides

3. Lower temperature to medium and add bell pepper, Spanish onion, garlic, hot sauce, mustard and cook for 3 minutes until veggies are tender

4. Sprinkle paprika, salt, pepper and serve

5. Enjoy!

Nutritional Values (Per Serving)

- Calories: 24
- Fat: 3 g
- Saturated Fat: 1 g
- Carbohydrates: 2 g
- Fiber: 0.8 g
- Sodium: 219 mg
- Protein: 40 g

Beef And Spinach Meatballs

Prep Time: 10 minutes

Cooking Time: 20 minutes

Number of Servings: 4

SmartPoints: 4

Ingredients:

- 1 cup onion
- 4 garlic cloves
- 1 whole egg
- 1 teaspoon oregano
- Salt and pepper to taste
- 3 cups lean ground beef
- 2 cups spinach

Method:

1. Preheat the oven to 360 degrees Fahrenheit.
2. In a mixing bowl, combine the remaining ingredients, mix well with your hands, and roll into meatballs.
3. Place on a baking sheet and bake for 20 minutes.
4. Enjoy!

<u>Nutritional Values (Per Serving)</u>

- Calories: 24

- Fat: 3 g

- Saturated Fat: 1 g

- Carbohydrates: 2 g

- Fiber: 0.8 g

- Sodium: 219 mg

- Protein: 40 g

Peppery- Beef Tenderloin

Prep Time: 10 minutes

Cooking Time: 20 minutes

Number of Servings: 4

SmartPoints: 4

Ingredients:

- 1 tablespoon olive oil

- 1 tablespoon rosemary, chopped

- 2 garlic cloves, sliced

- 1 tablespoon thyme, chopped

- 2 pounds beef tenderloin

- Salt and pepper to taste

- 1 tablespoon sage, chopped

Method:

1. Preheat your oven to 340 degrees F
2. Take a small knife and cut incisions on tenderloin; insert one slice of garlic into the incision
3. Rub meat with oil
   A. Take a bowl and add salt. sage, thyme, rosemary, pepper, and mix well
4. Rub spice mix over tenderloin

5. Put rubbed tenderloin into roasting pan and bake for 10 minutes

6. Lower temperature to 360 degrees F and cook for 20 minutes more until an internal thermometer read 140 degrees F

7. Transfer tenderloin to cutting board and let them sit for 15 minutes, slice into 20 pieces, and enjoy!

Nutritional Values (Per Serving)

- Calories: 183
- Fat:9g
- Carbohydrates: 15 g
- Protein: 24g
- Saturated Fat 3g
- Sodium: 2154mg
- Fiber: 1g

Juicy And Succulent French Pork Cutlets

Prep Time: 10 minutes

Cooking Time: 10 minutes

Number of Servings: 4

SmartPoints: 4

Ingredients:

- 1 tablespoon olive oil

- 2 pork cutlets

- 1 bell pepper, deveined and sliced

- 1 Spanish onion, chopped

- 2 garlic cloves, minced

- ½ teaspoon hot sauce

- ½ teaspoon mustard

- ½ teaspoon paprika

- Salt and pepper to taste

Method:

1. Put olive oil in a large saucepan and heat it over medium-high heat.

2. Allow to heat for 3-4 minutes, then add the pork cutlets and fry until golden and crispy on both sides.

3. Reduce the heat to medium and cook for 3 minutes, or until the bell pepper, Spanish onion, garlic, hot sauce, and mustard are tender.

4. Serve with paprika, salt, and pepper.

5. Enjoy!

Nutritional Values (Per Serving)

- Calories: 24

- Fat: 3 g

- Saturated Fat: 1 g

- Carbohydrates: 2 g

- Fiber: 0.8 g

- Sodium: 219 mg

- Protein: 40 g

Spaghetti Squash And Turkey Bolognese

Prep Time: 10 minutes

Cooking Time: 30-40 minutes

Number of Servings: 4

SmartPoints: 7

Ingredients:

- 1 carrot, peeled and chopped
- 4 garlic cloves, minced
- 1 large spaghetti squadh
- 1 pound lean ground turkey
- 1 tablespoon olive oil
- 1 onion, chopped
- 25 ounces marinara sauce
- Salt and pepper to taste

Method:

1. Preheat oven to 400 degrees. Cut the spaghetti squash lengthwise, and spoon out all the innards and seeds. Lightly mist with olive oil or cooking spray, and sprinkle with salt and pepper.

2. Place both halves cut side down on a baking sheet, and roast for 40 to 50 minutes, or until the flesh is very tender when poked with a fork. Allow squash to cool.

3. While squash is roasting, heat the oil in a large skillet over medium heat.

4. Add the onion and garlic and saute until translucent, about 5 minutes. Add the turkey, and saute until the meat is no longer pink. Add the carrot and saute until tender, about another 5 minutes.

5. Add the marinara sauce. Decrease the heat to medium-low and simmer gently for 15 minutes to allow the flavors to blend, stirring often. Season as desired with additional salt and pepper.

6. Using a fork, scrape out the strands from the inside of the spaghetti squash, and divide evenly into 4 servings. Top with bolognese sauce and serve immediately.

Nutritional Values (Per Serving)

- Calories: 274

- Fat: 2 g

- Saturated Fat: 1 g

- Carbohydrates: 3 g

- Fiber: 0.8 g

- Sodium: 222 mg

- Protein: 23 g

Classical London Broil Meal

Prep Time: 10 minutes

Cooking Time: 10 minutes

Number of Servings: 4

SmartPoints: 5

Ingredients:

- ¼ teaspoon pepper
- ½ teaspoon salt
- 1 tablespoon fresh rosemary, chopped
- 1 garlic clove, minced
- ½ cup red wine, dry
- 1 (1 pound) steak, top round, trimmed

Method:

1. Combine wine, garlic, rosemary, salt, and pepper in a large zip-close plastic bag

2. Add the steak

3. Squeeze out air and seal bag, turn to coat steak

4. Refrigerate, turning bag occasionally, at least 6 hours or up to overnight

5. Preheat broiler.

6. Remove steak from bag; discard marinade

7. Put the steak on broiler rack and broil 5 inches from heat until an instant-read thermometer inserted into the center of steak registers 145 degrees F, about 4 minutes per side

8. Transfer to cutting board; let stand 5 minutes

9. Cut across the grain into 16 slices.

10. Serve and enjoy!

Nutritional Values (Per Serving)

- Calories: 186

- Fat: 5 g

- Carbohydrate: 1 g

- Protein: 27 g

- Saturated fat: 2 g

- Fiber: 0 g

- Sodium: 327 mg

Lamb Cutlets Honey Glaze

Prep Time: 10 minutes

Cooking Time: 10 minutes

Number of Servings: 4

SmartPoints: 0

Ingredients:

- 1 tablespoon of Dijon mustard
- 1 tablespoon of honey
- 2 tablespoons of white wine vinegar
- 16 ounce of trimmed lamb frenched cutlet with fat trimmed
- 8 *ounces* of cooked brown quick rice
- 2 cups of finely shredded baby spinach leaves

Method:

1. Combine the honey, mustard, honey, and vinegar in a small bowl.
2. Preheat your grill to high heat.
3. Cook the cutlets for 2 minutes on each side or thoroughly cook.
4. Near the end of your cooking, brush them with half of the mustard mixture.
5. Meanwhile, prepare your brown rice in the microwave and cook it.
6. While the rice is still hot, stir in the spinach leaves.

7. Distribute the rice evenly among your serving plates, then top with the cutlets and the remaining mustard mixture.

Nutritional Values (Per Serving)

- Calories: 1570

- Fat: 17 g

- Carbohydrate: 55 g

- Protein: 54 g

- Saturated fat: 7 g

- Fiber: 2 g

- Sodium: 340 mg

Meaty Lasagna Soup

Prep Time: 10 minutes

Cooking Time: 10-20 minutes

Number of Servings: 6

SmartPoints: 7

Ingredients:

- 1 yellow onion, chopped ° kosher salt

- 1 lb. lean ground turkey sausage (I used Jennie-O) or 93% lean ground beef (points will be different!)

- 4 cloves garlic, minced

- 2 8 oz. can crushed tomatoes

- 1 tbsp. dried oregano

- 5 cups low-sodium chicken broth

- 8 oz. lasagna noodles, broke into 2" pieces

- 2 cups fat-free shredded mozzarella

Toppings (optional):

- Grated Parmesan, for garnish °, Torn fresh basil, for garnish

Method:

1. In a large skillet over medium heat, spray the bottom of the pan with cooking spray. Add onions and season with salt. Cook until tender and golden, 5 minutes, add sausage, and cook until no longer pink. Drain fat and return to pot.

2. Add garlic and stir until fragrant, 1 minute, then add crushed tomatoes and dried oregano.

3. Pour in chicken broth and bring to a simmer.

4. Add lasagna noodles and cook, occasionally stirring, until al dente, 10 minutes.

5. Add mozzarella and stir, letting melt into the soup.

6. Garnish with Parm and basil.

7. Serving size: 1 cup.

Nutritional Values (Per Serving)

- Calories: 277
- Fat: 11 g
- Carbohydrate: 21 g
- Protein: 21 g
- Saturated fat: 2 g
- Fiber: 3 g
- Sodium: 209 mg

Cool Baked Ziti

Prep Time: 10 minutes

Cooking Time: 20-30 minutes

Number of Servings: 4

SmartPoints: 8

Ingredients:

- 5 cups penne noodles

- 2 tablespoons light butter

- 2 tablespoons all-purpose flour

- 2 cups low-fat milk

- 6 ounces fat-free cream cheese

- ¼ cup Franks, wing sauce

- 1 tablespoons ranch seasoning

- 4 ounces Rotisserie chicken

- Chives for garnish

- ½ cup low-fat Colby Jack Cheese

Method:

1. Preheat the oven to 350 degrees Fahrenheit. Cook pasta until al dente in a large pot of salted boiling water. Return to the pot after draining.

2. To make the sauce, follow these steps: In a large skillet over medium heat, melt the butter. Whisk in the flour until it is completely combined. Cook for one minute. After that, whisk in the milk until it is completely combined and no clumps remain. Cook for 2 minutes, or until the sauce has thickened.

3. Break up the cream cheese with a wooden spoon until it is melted and combined. Stir in the Frank's and ranch seasoning until everything is well combined.

4. Stir in the chicken, chives, and cooked ziti until the pasta is completely coated. Bake for 15 minutes, or until the Colby jack cheese is melted and golden.

5. Serve with chives as a garnish.

6. Makes 8 servings (1 cup per serving).

Nutritional Values (Per Serving)

- Calories: 297

- Fat: 15 g

- Carbohydrate: 43 g

- Protein: 22 g

- Saturated fat: 4 g

- Fiber: 1 g

- Sodium: 254 mg

Weight Watchers Grilled Flank Steak

Prep Time: 10 minutes

Cooking Time: 60-70 minutes

Number of Servings: 4

SmartPoints: 4

Ingredients:

- 1 large red onion, peeled and sliced into ¼ inch thick rounds

- 1 teaspoon salt

- 1-1/2 pounds lean flank steak, trimmed

- ¼ teaspoon pepper

- 1 large garlic, minced

- 2 teaspoons dried oregano

- 1 tablespoon olive oil

- 3 tablespoons red wine vinegar

Method:

1. Combine the vinegar, oil, oregano, garlic, and pepper in a large Ziploc bag. Seal the bag after adding the steak, squeezing out as much air as possible. Turn the bag over and over to coat the steak in the marinade. Refrigerate for at least 1 hour and up to 4 hours before serving. If possible, turn the bag off every now and then.

2. Preheat your grill to medium-high heat when you're ready to cook the steak.

3. Remove the steak from the marinade and throw it away. Using 3/4 teaspoon salt, season the steak. Sprinkle the remaining 1/4 teaspoon salt over the onion and spray it with olive oil nonstick spray.

4. Turn the steak over after 6 minutes on the grill. Continue to grill for another 6 minutes, or until an instant-read thermometer inserted into the side of the steak registers 145F degrees.

5. Place the steak on a cutting board and set it aside. Cover with foil to keep the heat in and set aside for 10 minutes.

6. While the steak is resting, grill the onions for about 8 minutes, occasionally turning until they are tender.

7. Place the steak on a serving platter and thinly slice it against the grain into 18 slices. Add the onions on top.

Nutritional Values (Per Serving)

- Calories: 195
- Fat: 9 g
- Carbohydrate: 3 g
- Protein: 25 g
- Saturated fat: 2 g
- Fiber: 3 g
- Sodium: 398 mg

Chapter 5: Vegan And Vegetarian

Perfectly Baked Garbanzo Beans

Number of Servings: 4

Prep Time: 10 minutes

Cooking Time: Nil

SmartPoints: 5

Ingredients:

- 1 can garbanzo beans, chickpeas

- 1 tablespoon olive oil

- 1 teaspoon salt

- 1 teaspoon garlic powder

- ½ teaspoon paprika

Method:

1. Take your oven and pre-heat your oven to a temperature of 375 degrees F

2. Take a baking sheet and line it with parchment paper

3. Drain your garbanzo beans and rinse them well

4. Pat the bans dry and transfer to a large bowl, add olive oil, paprika, garlic powder, salt, and mix well

5. Transfer to your oven and bake for 20 minutes

6. Take them out and give the beans a shake, roast for 25 minutes more

7. Serve and enjoy!

Nutritional Values (Per Serving)

- Calories: 395

- Fat: 7g

- Carbohydrates: 42g

- Protein: 35g

- Saturated Fat: 2g

- Sodium: 315mg

- Fiber: 2g

The Classic Coleslaw

Number of Servings: 3

Prep Time: 10 minutes

Cooking Time: Nil

SmartPoints: 2

Ingredients:

- 1 cup white cabbage
- 1 tablespoon mayonnaise
- ½ teaspoon ground black pepper
- ½ teaspoon salt

Method:

1. Transfer the cabbage to a large salad bowl and shred it.
2. generously season with pepper and salt
3. Mix in the mayonnaise thoroughly. Serve and enjoy!

Nutritional Values (Per Serving)

- Calories: 40
- Fat: 5g
- Carbohydrates: 4g
- Protein: 0.6g

- Saturated Fat: 1g

- Sodium: 324mg

- Fiber: 1g

Fresh And Lovely Garden Walnut Salad

Number of Servings: 4

Prep Time: 10 minutes

Cooking Time: Nil

SmartPoints: 1

Ingredients:

- 1 cup arugula

- 2 tablespoons walnuts, chopped

- 1 tablespoon avocado oil

- ½ teaspoon sesame seeds

- 1 teaspoon lemon juice

- ½ teaspoon lemon zest, grated

- 1 tomato, chopped

Method:

1. Chop arugula roughly, transfer to the salad bowl

2. Add walnuts, sesame seeds, chopped tomatoes

3. Make the dressing by mixing up avocado oil, sesame seeds, lemon juice, grated lemon zest in a bowl

4. Pour dressing over salad, stir well

5. Serve and enjoy!

Nutritional Values (Per Serving)

- Calories: 71

- Fat: 6g

- Carbohydrates: 3g

- Protein: 2.7g

- Saturated Fat: 1g

- Sodium: 126mg

- Fiber: 1g

Exotic Baba Ghanoush

Number of Servings: 4

Prep Time: 10 minutes

Cooking Time: Nil

SmartPoints: 1

Ingredients:

- 1 tablespoon extra virgin olive oil
- 2 garlic cloves, minced
- ¾ teaspoon salt
- ¼ teaspoon black pepper
- 1 pound eggplant

Method:

1. Preheat the oven to 400 degrees Fahrenheit. Spray a baking sheet with nonstick spray and line it with foil.

2. Prick eggplant several times with a knife and place on a baking sheet. Bake for 45 minutes, turning once until softened.

3. Remove the skin and stem from the eggplant once it has cooled enough to handle.

4. Using a knife, cut the eggplant into chunks. Puree the eggplant in a food processor. Pulse in the remaining ingredients to combine. Serve immediately or keep refrigerated for up to 4 days in an airtight container.

Nutritional Values (Per Serving)

- Calories: 52

- Fat: 4 g

- Carbohydrate: 5 g

- Protein: 1 g

- Saturated fat: 0.1 g

- Fiber: 1 g

- Sodium: 221 mg

The Watermelon And Peach Medley

Number of Servings: 4

Prep Time: 10 minutes

Cooking Time: Nil

SmartPoints: 3

Ingredients:

- 1 (2-pound) piece seedless watermelon, rind removed and cut into ^3A inch dice

- ½ cup coarsely crumbled ricotta salsa or feta cheese

- 3 tablespoons champagne vinegar or white wine vinegar

- 2 large peaches, pitted and cut into 3/4-inch pieces

- 2 mini (Persian) cucumbers, thinly sliced

- 1 scallion (white and light green parts only), cut into very thin strips

Method:

1. Take a bowl and add all ingredients except salsa and scallion

2. Toss them together

3. Let stand 10 minutes

4. Sprinkle with cheese and scallion

5. Serve and enjoy!

<u>Nutritional Values (Per Serving)</u>

- Calories: 133

- Fat: 5 g

- Carbohydrate: 19 g

- Protein: 4 g

- Saturated fat: 3 g

- Fiber: 2 g

- Sodium: 359 mg

Classical Israeli Shakshuka

Number of Servings: 4

Prep Time: 10 minutes

Cooking Time: 30

SmartPoints: 1

Ingredients:

- 5 garlic cloves, minced
- 1 jalapeno, diced
- 1 teaspoon cumin
- Salt and pepper to taste
- 1 tablespoon tomato paste
- 1 teaspoon sweet paprika
- 8 ripe tomatoes, diced
- 1 red bell pepper, diced
- 1 medium onion, diced
- 6 whole eggs
- 1 tablespoon olive oil
- ½ cup fat-free veggie broth
- 1 teaspoon smoked paprika

Method:

1. Heat the olive oil in a large frying pan over medium-high heat, then add the onion and garlic. Cook for about 2-3 minutes, or until the vegetables are tender.

2. Cook, occasionally stirring, for another 3 minutes after adding the bell peppers.

3. Reduce the heat to medium. Combine the tomatoes, broth, jalapenos, tomato paste, paprikas, and cumin in a large mixing bowl. Stir everything together thoroughly. Cover the pan and cook the mixture for 15 minutes on low heat.

4. Reduce the heat to a low setting. Season to taste with salt and pepper. Allow simmering for another 5-7 minutes, uncovered, to allow the liquid to reduce.

5. Gently crack the eggs over the tomato mixture, one at a time, evenly spacing them on top of the sauce.

6. On top of the sauce, the eggs will be cooked over easily.

7. Cover the pan and cook for another 5 minutes until the eggs are the desired texture (runny, soft, or firm).

Nutritional Values (Per Serving)

- Calories: 271

- Fat: 14 g

- Carbohydrate: 24 g

- Protein: 15 g

- Saturated fat: 3 g

- Fiber: 2 g

- Sodium: 400 mg

Asparagus And Arugula Salad

Number of Servings: 4

Prep Time: 10 minutes

Cooking Time: Nil

SmartPoints: 3

Ingredients:

- 1/4 teaspoon salt

- 1 tablespoon olive oil

- 1 tablespoon lemon juice

- 2 teaspoons lemon zest, grated

- 2 scallions thinly sliced

- 1 cup grape tomatoes, halved

- 3 cups loosely packed baby arugula

- 1/8 teaspoon black pepper

- ½ cup reduced feta cheese, crumbled

Method:

1. Place asparagus in a steamer basket and place it over a large skillet; add 1 inch of boiling water

2. Cover and steam for 5 minutes until crispy

3. Rinse asparagus under cold water and let it cool

4. Combine asparagus, arugula, tomatoes, scallions, and mint in a bowl

5. Make the dressing by mixing lemon zest, juice, oil, salt, and pepper together

6. Drizzle dressing over salad and toss

7. Serve and enjoy!

Nutritional Values (Per Serving)

- Calories: 78

- Fat: 1 g

- Carbohydrate: 3 g

- Protein: 4 g

- Saturated fat: 0.1 g

- Fiber: 4 g

- Sodium: 272 mg

Low-Calorie Sheet Pan Tofu And Veggie

Number of Servings: 4

Prep Time: 10 minutes

Cooking Time: 20-30

SmartPoints: 2

Ingredients:

- 1 tablespoon cilantro, chopped

- 1 green onion, cleaned

- 1 and ½ cups snap peas

- 8 mini sweet pepper

- 2 teaspoons rice vinegar

- 2 teaspoons honey

- ½ teaspoon orange zest

- ¼ teaspoon Sriracha sauce

- 2 teaspoons sesame oil

- 2 teaspoons soy sauce

- 1 garlic clove, chopped

- ½ tablespoons ginger, chopped

- 14 ounces firm tofu, drained

Method:

1. In a medium mixing bowl, slice the tofu into 3/4-inch cubes.

2. Combine the ginger, garlic, soy sauce, sesame oil, sriracha, orange peel, honey, and vinegar in a separate bowl. Half of it should be poured over the tofu and gently mixed in. Refrigerate for up to 1 day after marinating for 20 minutes.

3. Preheat the oven to 400 degrees Fahrenheit. Using foil, line a baking pan and spray the foil.

4. Bake for 10 minutes with the marinated tofu on foil.

5. While the tofu bakes, combine the peppers and snap peas in a mixing bowl. Then, pour the remaining marinade over them, tossing to coat thoroughly. Place the vegetables in the baking pan in a single layer, if possible. Cook for another 20 minutes at 350°F.

6. Place in a serving dish after removing from the oven. Garnish with green onion and cilantro, if desired.

Nutritional Values (Per Serving)

- Calories: 160

- Fat: 80 g

- Carbohydrate: 11 g

- Protein: 5 g

- Saturated fat: 10 g

- Fiber: 2 g

- Sodium: 351 mg

Tomato And Sweet Cheese Salad

Number of Servings: 4

Prep Time: 10 minutes

Cooking Time: Nil

SmartPoints: 3

Ingredients:

- ½ cup lightly packed fresh flat-leaf parsley
- 1 sweet onion, cut into thin wedges
- ¼ teaspoon pepper
- ½ teaspoon salt
- 1 teaspoon Dijon mustard
- 4 teaspoons olive oil
- 1 tablespoon lemon juice
- 2 tablespoons white wine vinegar
- 2 ounces goat cheese, grumble

Method:

1. Make a dressing by whisking in vinegar, lemon juice, oil, mustard, salt, and pepper in a small-sized bowl

2. Toss tomatoes, onion, parsley in a large bowl, drizzle dressing, and toss well

3. Serve with a sprinkle of goat cheese on top

4. Enjoy!

Nutritional Values (Per Serving)

- Calories: 86

- Fat: 2 g

- Carbohydrate: 4 g

- Protein: 3 g

- Saturated fat: 0.1 g

- Fiber: 2 g

- Sodium: 257 mg

The Zero Point Cabbage Soup

Number of Servings: 4

Prep Time: 10 minutes

Cooking Time: 20-30 minutes

SmartPoints: 0

Ingredients:

- 3 cups non-fat vegetable broth
- 2 garlic cloves, minced
- 1 tablespoon tomato paste
- 2 cups cabbage, chopped
- ½ yellow onion
- ½ cup green beans
- ½ cup zucchini, chopped
- ½ teaspoon basil
- ½ teaspoon oregano
- Salt and pepper

Method:

1. Using nonstick cooking spray, coat the pot. Cook for 5 minutes with the onions, carrots, and garlic.

2. Toss in the broth, tomato paste, cabbage, green beans, basil, oregano, and season to taste with salt and pepper.

3. Simmer for 5-10 minutes, or until all of the vegetables are tender, then add the zucchini and continue to cook for another 5 minutes or so.

4. I've experimented with a few different approaches. Green beans are not included. In addition to the yellow onion, add chopped green onions.

5. Everything is excellent. You can use any vegetables you want.

Nutritional Values (Per Serving)

- Calories: 30
- Fat: 4 g
- Carbohydrate: 4 g
- Protein: 3 g
- Saturated fat: 2 g
- Fiber: 2 g
- Sodium: 351 mg

Chapter 6: Fish And Seafood Recipes

Hearty Fully Parm-ed Up Garlic Shrimp

Prep Time: 10 minutes

Cooking Time: 6-10 minutes

Number of Servings: 4

SmartPoints: 4 per 6 ounces

Ingredients:

- Salt and pepper to taste

- 1 lemon juice

- 1 teaspoon Italian seasoning

- ¼ cup parmesan, grated

- 3 garlic cloves, minced

- 1 and ¼ pounds raw shrimp, peeled and deveined

- 2 tablespoons olive oil

Method:

1. Pre-heat your oven to a temperature of 300 degrees F

2. Take your baking sheet and add shrimp, cheese, seasoning, garlic, olive oil, and toss well until nicely coated

3. Transfer to your pre-heated oven

4. Cook for 6-8 minutes

5. Serve and enjoy!

Nutritional Values (Per Serving)

- Calories: 139

- Fat: 7 g

- Saturated Fat: 2 g

- Carbohydrates: 2 g

- Fiber: 1 g

- Sodium: 643 mg

- Protein: 16 g

Healthy Mediterranean Tuna Salad

Prep Time: 10 minutes

Cooking Time: Nil

Number of Servings: 2

SmartPoints: 4

Ingredients:

- 1 tablespoon fresh flat-leaf parsley, chopped
- Salt and pepper to taste
- ¼ cup roasted red pepper, diced
- 2 tablespoons olive oil
- 1 Can Wild Selection Solid White Albacore
- 2 tablespoons capers
- 8 Kalamata olives, sliced

Method:

1. Add all ingredients to a mixing bowl and use a fork to break up the tuna and incorporate them all together.
2. Serve immediately or store leftovers in the refrigerator.

Nutritional Values (Per Serving)

- Calories: 241

- Fat: 4 g

- Saturated Fat: 1 g

- Carbohydrates: 12 g

- Fiber: 2 g

- Sodium: 251 mg

- Protein: 5 g

Shrimp And Cilantro Plate

Prep Time: 10 minutes

Cooking Time: 5 minutes

Number of Servings: 3

SmartPoints: 0

Ingredients:

- 1 and ¾ pounds shrimp, peeled and deveined
- 2 tablespoons fresh lime juice
- ½ teaspoon ground cumin
- ¼ teaspoon cumin, ground
- 1 tablespoon olive oil
- 1 and ¼ cups fresh cilantro, chopped
- 1 teaspoon lime zest
- ½ teaspoon salt
- ¼ teaspoon pepper

Method:

1. Toss shrimp, cumin, garlic, lime juice, and ginger in a large mixing bowl.
2. Add oil to a large nonstick skillet and heat over medium-high heat until the oil is hot.
3. Sauté for 4 minutes after adding the shrimp mixture.

4. Remove the pan from the heat and stir in the cilantro, lime zest, salt, and pepper.

5. Combine all ingredients in a large mixing bowl and serve immediately.

Nutritional Values (Per Serving)

- Calories: 177

- Fat: 6 g

- Saturated Fat: 2 g

- Carbohydrates: 3 g

- Fiber: 2 g

- Sodium: 650 mg

- Protein: 27 g

Garlic Dredged Lemon-y Mahi Mahi

Number of Servings: 3

Prep Time: 10 minutes

Cooking Time: 30 minutes

SmartPoints: 2

Ingredients:

- 1 tablespoon extra-virgin olive oil

- 3 garlic cloves, minced

- 4 pieces (4 ounces each) mahi-mahi fillets

- ½ teaspoon pepper

- Zest from 1 lemon

Method:

1. Take a skillet and place it over medium heat, add oil and let it heat up

2. Add garlic and Sauté until fragrant

3. Add fillets and season with pepper, lemon zest

4. Preheat your oven to 350 degrees F

5. Transfer fish to oven and bake for 30 minutes

6. Serve and enjoy once done!

<u>Nutritional Values (Per Serving)</u>

- Calories: 111

- Fat: 2g

- Carbohydrates: 2g

- Protein: 21g

- Saturated Fat: 1g

- Sodium: 162mg

- Fiber: 0.5g

Teriyaki One Pan Salmon

Number of Servings: 3

Prep Time: 10 minutes

Cooking Time: 10-15 minutes

SmartPoints: 9

Ingredients:

- 1 tablespoon sesame seeds

- 2 tablespoons scallions, chopped

- 1 and ½ tablespoons sesame oil

- 1 tablespoon salt

- 2 carrots, cut into small cubes

- 2 zucchini, cut into small cubes

- ½ pound salmon fillet

- ½ orange, sliced

- 2/3 cup pineapple cubed

- ½ tablespoon corn starch

- 2 garlic cloves

- 1 tablespoon ginger, peeled and cut into matchsticks

- ½ orange juiced

- 2 tablespoons honey

- ¼ cup mirin

- ½ cup soy sauce

Method:

1. Preheat the oven to 400 degrees Fahrenheit.

2. Bring the soy sauce, mirin, orange juice, and cornstarch to a boil in a pot over medium heat. Reduce the heat to low and stir in the pineapple until it thickens.

3. Place the salmon fillet skin-side down on a parchment-lined baking sheet and slide the orange halfway under the fillet.

4. Arrange the zucchini and carrots around the outside of the fillet.

5. Season with salt and sesame oil, then pour the marinade over the salmon fillet, reserving a small amount to finish the dish.

6. Bake for 15 minutes, then broil for 5 minutes, or until caramelized on top.

7. More sauce, scallions, and sesame seeds can be added as a garnish.

8. Enjoy over a bed of brown rice!

Nutritional Values (Per Serving)

- Calories: 277

- Fat: 8g

- Carbohydrates: 33g

- Protein: 22g

- Saturated Fat: 5g

- Sodium: 251mg

- Fiber: 2g

Fancy Greek Halibut

Prep Time: 10 minutes

Cooking Time: 30 minutes

Number of Servings: 6

SmartPoints: 4

Ingredients:

- 6 ounces halibut fillets
- 1 tablespoon Greek seasoning
- 1 large tomato, chopped
- 1 onion, chopped
- 5 ounces kalamata olives, pitted
- ¼ cup capers
- ¼ cup olive oil
- 1 tablespoon lemon juice
- Salt and pepper as needed

Method:

1. Preheat your oven to 350 degrees F
2. Transfer your fillets to a large-sized aluminum foil
3. Season them generously with Greek seasoning
4. Take a bowl and add onion, tomato, olives, olive oil, pepper, capers, lemon juice, salt

5. Mix well, then spoon the whole mixture over halibut

6. Seal the edges of the aluminum to form small packets

7. Transfer the packets to your baking sheet, bake for 30-40 minutes in your oven

8. Serve and enjoy once the fish shows a flaky texture!

Nutritional Values (Per Serving)

- Calories: 429

- Fat: 26 g

- Saturated Fat: 8 g

- Carbohydrates: 10 g

- Fiber: 2 g

- Sodium: 531 mg

- Protein: 36 g

Wholesome Skinny Tuna Salad

Prep Time: 10 minutes

Cooking Time: Nil

Number of Servings: 2

SmartPoints: 3

Ingredients:

- 2 romaine lettuce, optional

- 1 tablespoon lemon juice

- 1 tablespoon fresh dill, minced

- 3 tablespoons mayonnaise

- 3 tablespoons dried sweetened cranberries

- ¼ cup dried scallions

- 1/3 cup celery, chopped

- ½ cup apples, chopped

- 1 can white albacore tuna

Method:

1. Except for the lettuce, combine all ingredients in a mixing bowl. To combine, whisk everything together thoroughly.

2. 1 cup tuna, scooped into a small dish or bowl. Alternatively, place a romaine lettuce leaf on each plate. 1 cup tuna, spooned onto each lettuce leaf

Nutritional Values (Per Serving)

- Calories: 205

- Fat: 8 g

- Saturated Fat: 2 g

- Carbohydrates: 2 g

- Fiber: 1 g

- Sodium: 251 mg

- Protein: 11 g

Shrimp Scampi Zoodles

Prep Time: 10 minutes

Cooking Time: Nil

Number of Servings: 2

SmartPoints: 3

Ingredients:

- 1/8 teaspoon hot red pepper flakes

- 3 tablespoons lemon juice

- ½ teaspoon lemon zest, grated

- 1 tablespoon fresh parsley leaves, chopped

- Fresh ground pepper

- Salt as needed

- 12 large peeled and deveined shrimp

- 4 garlic cloves, minced

- 2 teaspoon extra virgin olive oil

- ½ tablespoons unsalted butter

- 2 medium zucchini

Method:

1. Use a mandolin fitted with a julienne blade or a spiralizer to zucchini into noodles.

Cut the strips into 6 to 8-inch strips.

2. Melt the butter and 1 teaspoon olive oil in a large nonstick pan over medium heat. Add the garlic and saute for 1 minute. Add the shrimp, kosher salt, and pepper and saute until the shrimp have just turned pink, about 5 minutes, stirring often. Set aside.

3. Add the remaining oil and garlic to the skillet, cook 30 seconds, then add the zucchini noodles, kosher salt, and pepper. Cook 2 minutes, stirring.

4. Remove from the heat, add the shrimp, parsley, lemon zest, lemon juice, and red pepper flakes. Toss well to combine and serve immediately.

5. Makes 2 servings. 6 shrimp, half the noodles.

Nutritional Values (Per Serving)

- Calories: 161
- Fat: 8 g
- Saturated Fat: 2 g
- Carbohydrates: 13 g
- Fiber: 2 g
- Sodium: 355 mg
- Protein: 4 g

Salmon With Cucumber Sauce

Prep Time: 10 minutes

Cooking Time: 5 minutes

Number of Servings: 4

Ingredients:

- 1 pound salmon steaks
- ½ cup plain low-fat Greek yogurt
- ½ cup cucumber, peeled and diced
- 1 tablespoon fresh dill, chopped
- 1 tablespoon olive oil
- ½ teaspoon ground coriander
- 1 teaspoon fresh lemon juice
- 1 cup water
- Salt and pepper to taste

Method:

1. Mix low-fat Greek yogurt, dill, cucumber, and a pinch of salt and pepper to taste, then chill.
2. Season salmon steaks with salt, pepper, coriander, and lemon juice after brushing them with olive oil.
3. Place a steamer rack on top of the water in the pot.

4. Place the fish fillets on the rack and close the lid.

5. Cook for 3 minutes on HIGH pressure.

6. Over ten minutes, let the pressure out naturally.

7. Serve salmon with cucumber sauce after opening the lid.

8. Enjoy!

Nutritional Values (Per Serving)

- Calories: 406

- Fat: 3g

- Carbohydrates: 6.5g

- Protein: 50g

- Saturated fat: 2g

- Fiber: 2g

- Sodium: 287 mg

86c3f5c3-eb94-457f-94d1-7125d07574a4R02